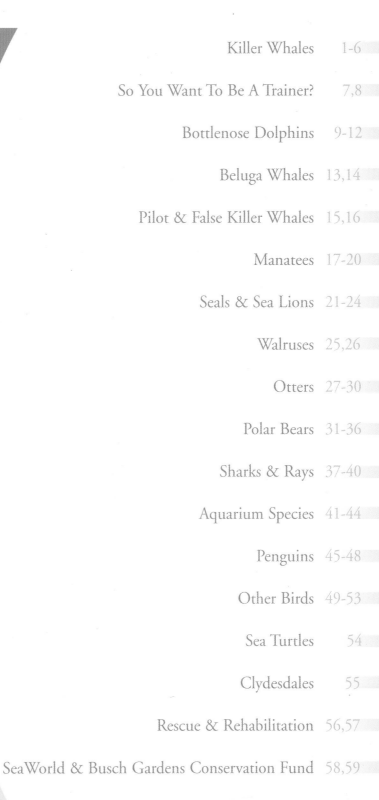

Killer Whales 1-6

So You Want To Be A Trainer? 7,8

Bottlenose Dolphins 9-12

Beluga Whales 13,14

Pilot & False Killer Whales 15,16

Manatees 17-20

Seals & Sea Lions 21-24

Walruses 25,26

Otters 27-30

Polar Bears 31-36

Sharks & Rays 37-40

Aquarium Species 41-44

Penguins 45-48

Other Birds 49-53

Sea Turtles 54

Clydesdales 55

Rescue & Rehabilitation 56,57

SeaWorld & Busch Gardens Conservation Fund 58,59

Up-Cl 50

# Killer Whales
## (*Orcinus orca*)

With Shamu as SeaWorld's most visible ambassador, killer whales are among our guests' favorite marine mammals. They belong to the order Cetacea along with all types of whales, dolphins and porpoises. Killer whales are the largest predators of warm-blooded mammals alive today. In addition to a diet consisting of various fishes, they are known to prey upon a wide variety of other animals such as squids, seals, sea lions, walruses, birds, sea turtles, otters, penguins, and even other whales (thus the name "killer whale").

Killer whales live in cohesive long term social units called pods. The size of a pod normally varies from fewer than 5 to about 30 individuals. Pods usually consist of males, females and calves of various ages. Females and juveniles usually remain in the center of the pod, while adult males swim in the wings.

A healthy adult has no natural predators, but sharks prey on older, younger and ill killer whales.

## Fast Facts:

* Adult males average 5.8 to 6.7 m (19-22 ft.) and usually weigh 3,628 to 5,442 kg (8,000-12,000 lb.).

* Adult females average 4.9 to 5.8 m (16-19 ft.) and usually weigh 1,361 to 3,628 kg (3,000-8,000 lb.).

* Killer whales have from 40 to 56 cone-shaped teeth in their mouths—their teeth are designed for grasping and tearing but not for chewing.

* Killer whales are actually the largest member of the dolphin family of Delphinidae.

* Despite living their entire lives in the water, whales are mammals and therefore more related to humans than to fish.

* At SeaWorld, our killer whales receive from 63.5 to 109 kg (140 to 240 lb.) of restaurant quality fish per day.

## BABY, OH BABY!

SeaWorld has the finest breeding program for killer whales of any zoological park on the planet. To date, we've had more than 20 successful births at our parks.

## Fast Facts:

- Killer whales are pregnant for up to 17 months.

- Calves average 2.6 m (8.5 ft.) and 136 to 181 kg (300-400 lb.) at birth.

- Calves nurse for about a year.

- With a milk fat content up to 48%, calves grow quickly. Some gain 454 kg (1,000 lb.) in twelve months.

- The first killer whale to be born and thrive at any zoological park occurred at SeaWorld Orlando on September 26, 1985. This whale has grown to have several calves of her own!

- The first killer whale calf conceived through artificial insemination (AI) was born at SeaWorld on September 1, 2001. His birth was the result of 15 years of research on killer whale reproductive biology. The second calf was born May 3, 2002. Both AI-conceived calves were born at SeaWorld San Diego, but the father was 3,000 miles away at SeaWorld Orlando.

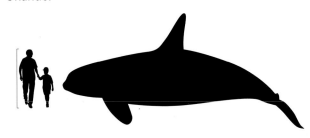

# So You Want to be a Trainer?

Animal trainers have one of the most visible and desired jobs in a zoological park. At SeaWorld, animal trainers work with birds, sea lions, walruses, otters, dolphins and other whales—including Shamu!

Few colleges offer an animal training degree, but degrees in other fields such as animal behavior, psychology or zoology are useful. To help become a good performer, future trainers may choose an educational background in drama or communications.

Opportunities for animal trainers are very limited. For every opening there may be dozens of qualified applicants. It's not easy to work with killer whales and other animals at SeaWorld, but it's a very rewarding job.

Those who wish to be trainers should maintain good grades in school, develop swimming skills as much as possible, take scuba classes, practice public speaking abilities and maintain a positive attitude. Our trainers have one simple piece of advice to anyone out there who aspires to become a trainer one day—*believe and you will achieve!*

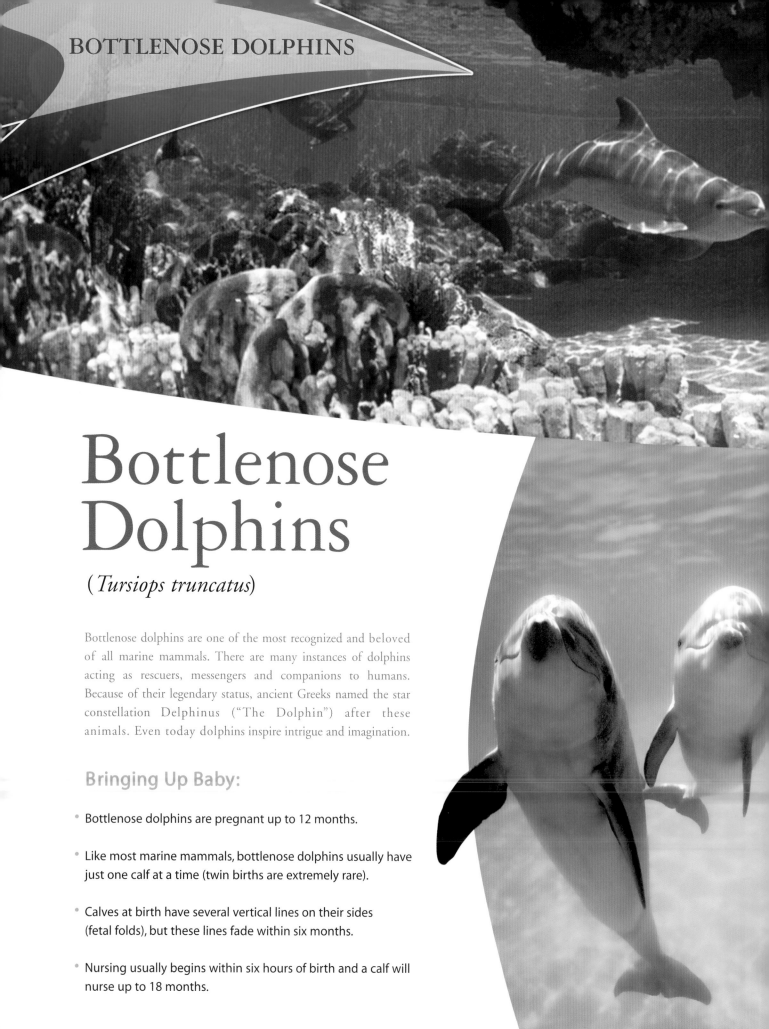

# Bottlenose Dolphins

## (*Tursiops truncatus*)

Bottlenose dolphins are one of the most recognized and beloved of all marine mammals. There are many instances of dolphins acting as rescuers, messengers and companions to humans. Because of their legendary status, ancient Greeks named the star constellation Delphinus ("The Dolphin") after these animals. Even today dolphins inspire intrigue and imagination.

## Bringing Up Baby:

* Bottlenose dolphins are pregnant up to 12 months.

* Like most marine mammals, bottlenose dolphins usually have just one calf at a time (twin births are extremely rare).

* Calves at birth have several vertical lines on their sides (fetal folds), but these lines fade within six months.

* Nursing usually begins within six hours of birth and a calf will nurse up to 18 months.

## Fast Facts:

* Bottlenose dolphins belong in the same scientific family of Delphinidae as killer whales.

* Bottlenose dolphin adults average 2.5 to 3 m (8–10 ft.) and weigh between 136 and 295 kg (200–650 lb.).

* They are protected by several laws although they are not considered endangered or threatened.

* They have been seen jumping as high as 4.9 m (16 ft.) out of the water and landing on their backs or sides in a behavior called a breach.

* Both young and old dolphins chase one another and toss, carry or use objects to solicit interaction with other dolphins.

# Beluga Whales
### (*Delphinapterus leucas*)

The English name "beluga" comes from the Russian word belukha, which means "white." Belugas are also known as white whales. The white coloration helps protect belugas from predators by camouflaging them among the icebergs and ice floes of the northern seas. However, at birth beluga calves are generally dark gray. They gradually lighten with age and upon reaching maturity (about eight or nine years for males), attain the white coloration characteristic of adult belugas.

Typically, beluga whales inhabit shallow coastal waters of the icy Arctic Ocean and its adjoining seas, but during the summer many populations may also congregate in warmer freshwater estuaries and river basins.

## Fast Facts:

- Beluga whales are toothed whales from the family Monodontidae (the only other member of this family is the narwhal). They have many unique features which is why they are classified in a different family than most other whales.

- Beluga whales are among the few whales that have unfused neck vertebrae—this feature makes their necks quite flexible and gives their heads a wide range of motion.

- They're also called "sea canaries" for the wide range of sounds belugas can make.

- Belugas can swim forward as well as backwards— a rarity among whales.

- Expensive beluga caviar comes from the beluga sturgeon fish (*Huso huso*), not from the beluga whale.

# False Killer &
## (*Pseudorca crassidens*)

When seen by humans from a distance, this whale may look like its close relative, the killer whale. When viewed up close, it can be seen that false killer whales are mostly black in color. The bottom (ventral) side of the animal varies in color from gray to white.

Male false killer whales average 5.3 m (17.6 ft.) in length and may weigh up to 2,200 kg (4,800 lb.). Females average 4.5 m (15 ft.) in length and may weigh up to 1,200 kg (2,600 lb.). The longest recorded male was 5.9 m (19 ft.) while the longest female was 5.1 m (17 ft.).

## Fast Facts:

* False killer whales prey upon a variety of large animals including cod, yellowtail tuna, and squid. Their diet may include other cetaceans-they have been observed attacking dolphins entangled in seine nets.

* The false killer whale is thought to inhabit all tropical, subtropical, and warm temperate seas. There have also been sightings reported off the Atlantic coast of Maryland, north Argentina and also the northern coasts of the British Isles.

# Pilot Whales
## (*Globicephala melas*)

The roundheaded, dark gray or pilot whale earned its nickname from fishermen who believed that these whales piloted them to schools of fish. Pilot whales are a commonly seen whale species since they swim in all of the world's oceans.

Pilot whales are the second largest member of the Delphinidae family (next to the killer whale), with mature males being as much as twice the weight of mature females.

## Fast Facts:

- Pilot whales primarily feed upon squid, although cuttlefish, octopuses and small types of fishes such as herring are also part of their diet.

- Like other whales, they are protected in the United States by the Marine Mammal Protection Act of 1972.

# Manatees
## (Family Trichechidae)

Manatees belong to the mammalian order Sirenia. Believe it or not, they were once thought to be the mythological sirens that would sing out to sailors in order to lure the doomed crew into wrecking their boats along rocky shorelines. Another legend that grew from manatees is the story of mermaids. Of course, manatees are neither sirens nor mermaids, but rather gentle marine mammals that are found in just a few parts of the world.

There are three species of manatee: the Amazon manatee (*Trichechus inunguis*); the West African manatee (*Trichechus senegalensis*); and the West Indian manatee (*Trichechus manatus*). Scientists also recognize two subspecies of West Indian manatee: the Florida manatee (*T. m. latirostris*) and the Antillean manatee (*T. m. manatus*). The order Sirenia has one other living species, the dugong. A fifth species, the Steller's sea cow, was hunted to extinction by 1768, a mere 27 years after they were first discovered. All manatees are either threatened or endangered, and they are protected by legislation in every country where they are found.

Manatees inhabit the tropical and sub–tropical waters of North and South America and Africa. The West Indian and West African manatees live in rivers, bays, estuaries, and coastal areas. They can move freely between freshwater and saltwater habitats. The Amazonian manatee is restricted to the freshwater Amazon basin.

Florida manatees average 3 m (10 ft.) and weigh 363 to 544 kg (800–1,200 lb.) A female manatee, called a cow, gives birth about once every three years. The gestation period is about 12 months. At birth, West Indian manatees measure about 1.2 to 1.4 m (4–5 ft.) and weigh 27 to 32 kg (60–70 lb.). The calf nurses from teats under the mother's pectoral flippers.

Florida manatees are highly susceptible to cold and it's not unusual for them to die during extremely cold weather. But human impact from boating, entanglement in fishing line, poaching and habitat destruction pose a great threat to manatees as well.

## Fast Facts:

- Manatees are herbivores, feeding on aquatic vegetation. For this reason they are sometimes referred to as sea cows.

- Florida manatees feed on more than 60 varieties of plants.

- The extinct Steller's sea cow was reported to be some 9.2 m (30 ft.) in length.

- Rescued manatees are on display to educate the public at both SeaWorld Orlando and SeaWorld San Diego.

# Harbor

## (*Phoca vitulina*)

The harbor seal is probably the most wide-ranging and abundant pinniped. Four subspecies inhabit northern Pacific and Atlantic coastlines. A fifth subspecies, *Phoca vitulina mellonae*, is a landlocked group of harbor seals living in freshwater Seal Lake in Quebec, Canada. The most abundant subspecies is *P. v. richardsi*–an estimated 200,000 individuals inhabit the eastern North Pacific from the Pribilof Islands of Alaska to Baja California, Mexico.

Male harbor seals reach lengths of about 2 m (6.6 ft.) and weigh as much as 170 kg (375 lb.). Females are slightly smaller, measuring up to 1.7 m (5.6 ft.) and weighing in at about 150 kg (331 lb.). When born, the well-developed pups measure up to 100 cm (39 in.) and weighs up to 12 kg (26 lb.).

Unlike most other pinnipeds, harbor seals are generally solitary and rarely interact with one another. When hauled out, adults maintain a meter or more (several feet) between them. Harbor seals are not highly communicative but if threatened a seal may respond by snorting, growling, lunging, scratching, or other aggressive gestures.

# Seals

## Fast Facts:

- Harbor seals exhibit a wide range of color variations, from silver with black spots, to black with gray rings, to almost pure white.

- Harbor seals swim with alternate back-and-forth movements of their hind flippers.

- They can remain submerged for up to 28 minutes and dive to depths of 90 m (295 ft.), however, they routinely forage in shallow waters.

- Harbor seals feed on squid, crustaceans, molluscs and fishes.

# California
## (*Zalophus californianus californianus*)

Male California sea lions establish breeding territories on beaches from May to July along the coasts of Southern California and Baja California. These breeding areas, called rookeries, are noisy places. Males bark incessantly when defending their established territories. A male with an established territory breeds with an average of 16 females in one season.

Most pups are born in late June. Newborns are about 80 cm (2.6 ft.) long and weigh 6 to 9 kg (13.2–19.8 lb). Adult males are 2 to 2.5 m (6.5–8.2 ft.) long and weigh 200 to 400 kg (441–882 lb.). Females are 1.5 to 2 m (5–6.6 ft.) long and weigh 50 to 110 kg (110–243 lb.).

Several days after the pup's birth, the mother leaves the pup in the crowded rookery as she searches for food in the ocean. When she returns, the mother emits a loud trumpeting vocalization, which elicits a bleating response from her pup. This exchange continues until mother and pup find each other. She makes her final identification by smelling her own pup.

## Seals vs. Sea Lions

Many people confuse seals and sea lions as they share many similarities. They are both members of the order Pinnipedia, which means "feather footed." Pinnipeds have a substantial system of nerves in their upper lips and use thick whiskers called vibrissae to find food. Their hearing and eyesight are adapted for underwater and their acute sense of smell helps females identify their pups. Most of a pinniped's life is spent in water, although they will come ashore (haul out) to rest or lie in the sun.

When in doubt, here's an easy guide to tell California sea lions apart from harbor seals:

### California sea lions
- Generally more social, living in larger groups
- Vocal and noisy
- Paddlelike hind flippers can be rotated forward to move across land more easily
- Ear flaps

### Harbor seals
- Usually more solitary
- Tend to be more quiet and shy
- Cannot rotate hind flippers under body, so instead they pull themselves across land
- No visible ear flaps, just small pinhole openings behind the eyes

# Sea Lions

## Fast Facts:

* California sea lions inhabit rocky and sandy beaches of coastal islands and mainland shorelines.

* On land, they gather in large groups called colonies or rookeries. In water, California sea lions form smaller groups called rafts.

* Sea lions have loud roars, which may explain why they are named after lions that live on land. Male sea lions of some species even grow a thick mane around their necks.

* Sea lions eat squids, octopuses and a variety of fishes. In turn, they are hunted by killer whales and sharks.

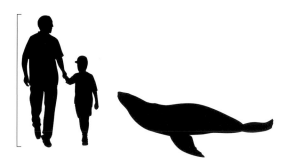

# Walruses

## (*Odobenus rosmarus*)

Walruses spend about two-thirds of their lives in the water. Herds of walruses haul out (leave the water to go on land) on sea ice to rest and bear their young. They prefer snow-covered moving pack ice or ice floes but they also haul out on small rocky islands when ice isn't present. Most walruses live where the air temperature is about -15º to +5ºC (+5ºC to 41ºF).

Male walruses weigh about 800 to 1,700 kg (1,764–3,748 lb.). Females weigh about 400 to 1,250 kg (882–2,756 lb.). Atlantic walruses are slightly smaller than Pacific walruses.

A lot of this weight comes from the thick layer of blubber that insulates the walrus from the cold. Blubber may be up to 15 cm (6 in.) thick. During the winter, blubber may account for one third of a walrus' total body mass. Blubber also streamlines the body and functions as an excess energy reserve.

A walrus is a big animal with a big appetite—some at SeaWorld eat around 36 kg (80 lb.) of food per day! They prefer to eat bivalve molluscs such as clams. Walruses may also eat many other kinds of invertebrates including worms, snails, squids and crabs. Although it is rare, some feed on seals.

To locate food, walruses use their vibrissae (whiskers). A walrus has about 400 to 700 vibrissae in 13 to 15 rows on its snout. Vibrissae are attached to muscles and are supplied with blood and nerves. A walrus moves its snout through bottom sediment to find food. Abrasion patterns of the tusks show that they are dragged through the sediment, but are not used to dig up prey. Walruses may also take in mouthfuls of water and squirt powerful jets at the sea floor, excavating burrowing invertebrates such as clams.

## Fast Facts:

* Walruses navigate like sea lions, steering in the water with their fore flippers and rotating their hind flippers to walk on all fours when on land.

* Walruses have been hunted as a food source but they have largely been killed for their ivory tusks. The Pacific walrus has been hunted to near-extinction and allowed to recover several times.

* Their tusks help them haul out of the water onto ice but mainly they are used to establish social dominance.

* Tusks can grow to a length of 100 cm (39 in.) in males and 80 cm (31.5 in.) in females. Tusks grow for about 15 years, although they may continue to grow in males.

* Since 1941, all U. S. commercial hunting has been banned with earlier protection given by Russia and Canada. However, indigenous people of the Arctic are permitted to have limited subsistence hunts of walruses.

# Otters
## (Family Mustelidae)

Sea otters (*Enhydra lutris*) once lived along most of the coastal North Pacific Ocean, before fur traders hunted them for their thick, luxurious pelts. By 1900, sea otters were nearly extinct. Today they are protected. The California population is still small—about 2,000 sea otters are spread over only about 226 km (140 mi.) of central California coastline. California sea otters are listed as "threatened" under the Endangered Species Act.

The sea otters' brown to black fur is the finest and densest of any animal fur. On a large animal, there are an estimated 650,000 hairs per square inch. A sea otter relies on its fur to keep it warm—it does not have blubber as other marine mammals do. Natural oils in a sea otter's fur repel water and trap tiny air bubbles, providing a layer of warm air between the otter's skin and the harsh elements of its environment.

Because they rely on their dense fur for insulation from the chilly ocean water, sea otters are particularly vulnerable to the detrimental effects of an oil spill. If a sea otter swims into an oil spill, the fur becomes soiled and loses its insulating qualities, allowing water to penetrate to the skin and causing hypothermia and ultimately, death.

The Asian small-clawed otters (*Aonyx cinerea*) and North American river otters (*Lutra canadensis*) are quick and agile members of the weasel family. Both types of river otters live in wetlands or along lakes, rivers, streams and ocean bays, burrowing under roots and logs to make their homes. Because river otters are solitary animals, pups strike out on their own within a year. Their diet includes fish, frogs, snakes, turtles, salamanders, shellfish, aquatic insects, larvae, snails, worms and ducks. On land, they will eat mice, small rabbits, ground-nesting birds and their eggs, and, if food is scarce, muskrats and young beavers.

River otters use their dexterous paws to feel for prey, handle small objects and swim. Their powerful tails act as rudders when the otter is swimming and as a brace when the animal stands on its hind paws. Hearing and smell are well developed, but their sight is better under water than on land.

North American river otters range from 100 to 153 cm (39-60 in.). The Asian small-clawed otter is the smallest of all otters, measuring 65 to 94 cm (26-37 in.) and weighing 1 to 5 kg (2.2-11 lb.).

## Fast Facts:

- Sick, injured or old river otters may fall victim to bobcats, lynxes, coyotes, wolves and large reptiles while pups are sometimes eaten by great horned owls.

- Sea otters spend up to 48% of the daylight hours grooming their fur. They groom by rubbing fur with their forepaws. Their strong claws comb and rake the fur. Then they roll and whirl in the water to smooth their fur.

- Sea otters sleep, rest, and usually swim on their backs. California sea otters spend almost all of their time in the water. Alaska sea otters often sleep, groom, and nurse on land.

- A decade after the devastating oil spill in Prince William Sound, SeaWorld San Diego, along with the California Department of Fish and Game and the University of California, Davis, broke ground on the SeaWorld Oiled Wildlife Care Center. Today SeaWorld is an important center for the rescue and rehabilitation of sea otters and other animals affected by oil spills.

# Polar Bears

## (*Ursus maritimus*)

Polar bears are powerful predators adapted for the cold. The fur of a polar bear can vary from pure white to creamy yellow to light brown depending upon the season and angle of light. A polar bear's skin is black to absorb sunlight and to help them stay warm. A thick layer of fat (blubber), up to 11 cm (4.3 in.) thick, keeps the polar bear warm even in ice cold water.

Adult male polar bears (boars) weigh from 350 to 650 kg (772–1,433 lb.) and are about 2.5 to 3 m (8.2–9.8 ft.) long. Adult female bears (sows) weigh from 150 to 250 kg (331–551 lb.) and are 2 to 2.5 m (6.6–8.2 ft.) long.

Polar bears are the largest living land carnivores, although they start life only weighing between 454 to 680 g (16–24 oz.) on the average. Polar bear cubs are born November through January in a den. At birth, cubs are only about 30 cm (12 in.) long. They are born small and helpless with their eyes closed and appear hairless because of their very fine fur. Cubs open their eyes within the first month and begin walking at two months. Cubs will not emerge from the den until they are four to six months old. They grow quickly and by eight months weigh over 45 kg (99 lb.). Young cubs have been seen chasing and tackling their siblings.

## Fast Facts:

- Adult polar bears need an average of 2 kg (4.4 lb.) of fat per day to maintain their weight. Their diet includes seals, walruses, whales, fishes and vegetation.

- Polar bears have amazing strength. They are capable of traveling 30 km (19 mi.) or more per day for several days. One polar bear was tracked traveling 80 km (50 mi.) in 24 hours. In water, some have been tracked swimming continuously for 100 km (62 mi.) while on land they can run as fast as 40 kph (25 mph).

- Polar bears are considered marine mammals because they are strong swimmers, using their front paws to propel themselves through the water dog-paddle style. The hind feet and legs are held flat and are used as rudders.

# Sharks

Sharks are some of the most amazing and misunderstood animals on the planet.

Sharks are a type of fish. Like other fish species, sharks and their close relatives (rays, skates, guitarfish and sawfish) have fins, live in the water and breathe with gills. Sharks and their relatives differ from the majority of fishes since they have a skeleton of cartilage instead of hard bone. Sharks and their relatives compose the class Chondrichthyes. Sharks are further separated into the superorder Selachii.

The characteristic teeth of each species are adapted to that particular species' diet. The teeth may be serrated, smooth or flat. Most are used for seizing prey, cutting or crushing. Sharks eat far less than most people imagine. In fact, in a zoological environment, a shark eats about 1% to 10% of its total body weight each week whereas a human may eat 2% to 3% of its body weight per day. Some sharks may go months without eating at all.

Only 32 of about 355 shark species have been known to attack humans. Like other wild animals, most sharks tend to avoid people. Sharks that have attacked probably mistook humans for other animals such as sea lions or they may have attacked to protect their territory. The majority of people that are attacked by sharks survive and only about 5 to 10 shark fatalities are reported in a year.

People have used sharks for medicines and food; shark teeth for weapons and jewelry; and shark skin for sandpaper. But today, some shark populations are threatened with extinction due to massive overfishing. The United States has passed laws to limit the amount of sharks killed each year in U.S. waters, but such regulations are rare in many countries.

## Fast Facts

- Sharks live all over the world, from warm, tropical lagoons to polar seas. Some even inhabit freshwater lakes and rivers.

- The largest shark, and the biggest fish alive today, is the whale shark (*Rhiniodon typus*) which can reach a length of up to 18 m (59 ft.). Perhaps the smallest species is the male pygmy shark (*Squaliolus laticaudus*) which may only reach a length of 15 cm (5.9 in.).

- Many shark species have a fusiform body shape (rounded and tapered at both ends). This body shape reduces drag and requires minimum energy to swim.

- Because of the biting force exerted by sharks (some up to 8,000 pounds per square inch) and the lack of a hard jaw bone to anchor the teeth in place, teeth often break off while sharks are feeding. They are replaced by teeth in reserve rows. The lemon shark (*Negaprion brevirostris*) can replace a tooth in about eight days.

- The smalltooth sawfish *(Pristis pectinata)* is a relative of sharks and is found in tropical Atlantic waters. The sawfish may swing its rostrum back and forth while swimming through a school of fish, injuring them from the impact. Sawfish have also been seen using their snout teeth to move sand around in search of invertebrates.

# Rays

All rays belong to the superorder Batoidea, which includes stingrays, electric rays, skates, guitarfish and sawfish. Like sharks–their closest relatives–batoids have skeletons made of tough connective tissue called cartilage. About 480 species of batoids are distributed worldwide, particularly in warm and temperate climates, and are found in oceans, estuaries, streams, lagoons, lakes, shallow offshore waters and along coastlines.

Reminiscent of birds in flight, some rays gently flap their enlarged pectoral fins, or "wings," to "fly" through and sometimes even leap out of the water. A ray's wingspan, or disc-size, can range from about 30 cm (12 in.) in yellow stingrays to more than 6.1 m (20 ft.) in manta rays.

Among the best known rays are stingrays, which have long, slim, whiplike tails armed with serrated, venomous spines. A stingray lashes its tail mostly when it is frightened, caught, stepped on or otherwise disturbed.

In many parts of the world, some rays are commercially important food sources, yet currently, rays are not considered endangered or threatened. Due to humankind's impact on the marine environment, concern is mounting for the future of rays throughout their range.

## Fast Fact:

- When wading in shallow waters, people should shuffle their feet to avoid stepping on a buried stingray (this is referred to as "The Stingray Shuffle").

- Rays give live birth to their young.

- Rays primarily feed on molluscs, crustaceans, worms and occasionally small fish.

- Some rays crush their prey between their blunt teeth, which are sometimes referred to as bony plates.

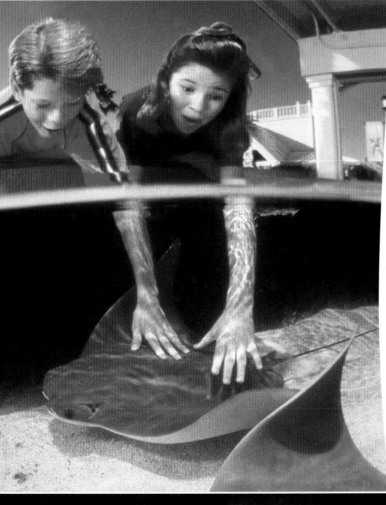

# Aquarium Species

SeaWorld is home to some of the world's most fascinating aquarium species. Here are some examples of some of the most interesting animals found at the SeaWorld parks:

**Groupers** can grow to incredible sizes, such as with the goliath grouper (*Epinephelus itajara*) of the tropical Atlantic Ocean. It can reach sizes of more than 3 m (10 ft.) long and a weigh greater than 453.6 kg (1,000 lb.). Groupers may undergo a sex reversal as they age, as in the case of yellowmouth groupers (*Mycteroperca interstitialis*). All young yellowmouth groupers are females, but as they grow larger they will change into a male.

**Seahorses** and **sea dragons** are found in temperate and tropical waters. A female seahorse deposits 100 or more eggs into a pouch on the male's abdomen. The male releases sperm into the pouch, fertilizing the eggs. The embryos develop within the male's pouch, nourished by their individual yolk sacs. Incubation may last two to six weeks, depending on the species. After the embryos have developed, the male gives birth to tiny seahorses, some as small as 1 cm (0.4 in.) long.

**Parrotfishes** have thick, heavy bodies and large scales. The teeth of a parrotfish are fused together, like a beak, to scrape algae and invertebrates from hard surfaces. Then, to crush

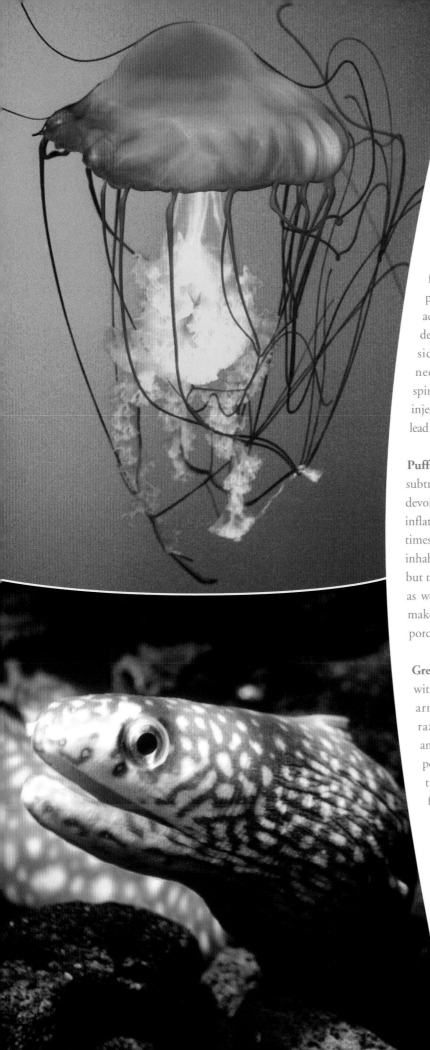

the ingested materials, they have pharyngeal teeth on the floor and roof of their throats. Parrotfishes graze over a reef much like a herd of cattle over a grassy field. Large amounts of calcareous materials are consumed and excreted by schools of parrotfishes when they feed, so these animals are a major factor in reef sediment redistribution. In just a single year, one parrotfish may turn a ton of coral into sand.

The delicate-looking **lionfish** shows little fear of intruders, for its feathery dorsal fin is well armed. A lionfish has a color pattern of contrasting reds and whites. These vivid colors may act as a warning to potential enemies to stay away from its deadly spines. When threatened, a lionfish turns its body sideways so any aggressor gets a painful jab from its needle-sharp spines. A lionfish can have up to 18 dorsal spines, some of which can be as long as 35.5 cm (14 in.). Once injected, the venom causes intensely painful wounds that can lead to convulsions, paralysis, and possibly even death to humans.

**Puffers** (family Tetraodontidae) can be found in tropical and subtropical oceans around the world. Those in this family are devoid of scales over much of their bodies. If alarmed, they can inflate themselves with water or air and balloon up to three times their normal size. **Porcupinefishes** (family Diodontidae) inhabit worldwide tropical seas. They too can inflate themselves, but these fishes have well-developed spines covering their bodies as well. These spines, which can be up to 5 cm (2 in.) long, make it even more challenging for a predator to bite into a porcupinefish.

**Great barracudas** (*Sphyraena barracuda*) are muscular fish with streamlined torpedo-shaped bodies. The most lethal armament of great barracudas is their impressive set of razor-sharp teeth. The lower jaw juts out past the upper jaw and both are filled with dozens of teeth. Some of these teeth point backwards to prevent slippery fish from escaping once they are seized. Great barracudas have a reputation of following human divers, which can be unnerving considering some individuals grow to 3 m (10 ft.) in length.

**Moray eels** also have a nasty reputation among divers exploring reef areas—a moray eel appears dangerous because it continually exposes its mouth and teeth. This action, however, is not hostile but simply the way an eel breathes. Generally, they are not known to be aggressive to divers unless disturbed or frightened. A mistake that some divers make is to use rocky areas as a hand hold, which may turn out to be home to several moray eels.

Such an action may frighten a moray eel to lash out and bite in self defense. Like many other "dangerous" sea creatures, they usually do not bite unless first provoked.

**Jellyfish** are related to sea anemones, hydras, and corals. Their bodies consist of two tissue layers; the outer epidermis, and the inner gastrodermis. A jellylike material, the mesoglea, lies between the tissue layers. This is the "jelly" that gives this animal its name. Jellyfish are infamous for their stinging tentacles, especially the highly dangerous box jellyfish in the order Cubomedusae. Normally, jellyfish may cause painful rashes to human skin but the stings from box jellyfish have been responsible for numerous human fatalities around Australia and the Philippines.

**Octopi** are among the 100,000+ types of molluscs in the huge phylum Mollusca. This advanced and complex invertebrate predator is further grouped in the class Cephalopoda along with nautiluses and squids. There are approximately 150 species of octopi and they are found worldwide in tropical and temperate oceans. Although most species span only between 30 to 60 cm (1–2 ft.), some can grow as large 10 m (30 ft.).

# Penguins

## (Family Speniscidae)

Penguins live only in Earth's southern hemisphere, from the warm equator to the chilly South Pole. Despite their comical antics, penguins thrive in some of the harshest environments on the planet. Feathers provide waterproofing critical to penguins' survival in water that may be as cold as -2.2°C (28°F) in the Antarctic. A thick layer of blubber also helps to insulate penguins from the cold.

Penguins come in many different sizes. The emperor penguin is the largest of all living penguins, standing 1.1 m (3.7 ft.) and weighing 27 to 41 kg (60–90 lb.). The smallest of the penguins is the fairy penguin (*Eudyptula minor*), standing just 41 cm (16 in.) and weighing about 1 kg (2.2 lb.). Some extinct species of penguins were believed to be incredibly large. One species, *Anthropomis nordenskjoldi*, may have stood 1.5 to 1.8 m (5–5.9 ft.) and weighed 90 to 135 kg (198–298 lb.)!

Penguins are superb swimmers and depend upon the sea for their food. They move their flippers up and down to soar through the sea in a motion that resembles the wing movements of flying birds. They use their short tails and feet like a boat's rudder to steer. Penguins typically dive 15.3 to 18.3 m (50-60 ft.) to find food. Most penguins eat fishes, squids and krill. A penguin's striking black and white feathers provide camouflage as it swims.

Penguins have no natural land predators, although predatory birds may take eggs and chicks. In the water, penguin predators include leopard seals, fur seals, sea lions and occasionally killer whales or sharks.

Penguin species found at the SeaWorld Adventure Parks include the emperor (*Aptenodytes forsteri*), king (*Aptenodytes patagonicus*), Adélie (*Pygoscelis adeliae*), chinstrap (*Pygoscelis antarctica*), gentoo (*Pygoscelis papua*), macaroni (*Eudyptes chrysolophus*), rockhopper (*Eudyptes chrysocome*) and Magellanic (*Spheniscus magellanicus*).

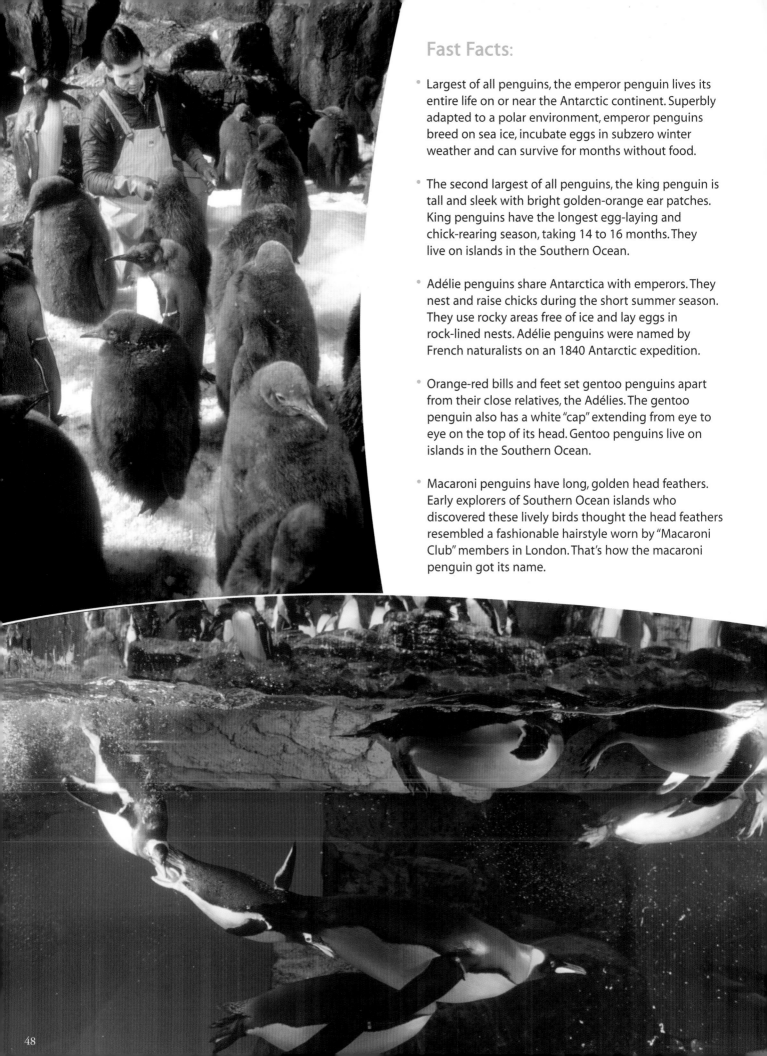

## Fast Facts:

- Largest of all penguins, the emperor penguin lives its entire life on or near the Antarctic continent. Superbly adapted to a polar environment, emperor penguins breed on sea ice, incubate eggs in subzero winter weather and can survive for months without food.

- The second largest of all penguins, the king penguin is tall and sleek with bright golden-orange ear patches. King penguins have the longest egg-laying and chick-rearing season, taking 14 to 16 months. They live on islands in the Southern Ocean.

- Adélie penguins share Antarctica with emperors. They nest and raise chicks during the short summer season. They use rocky areas free of ice and lay eggs in rock-lined nests. Adélie penguins were named by French naturalists on an 1840 Antarctic expedition.

- Orange-red bills and feet set gentoo penguins apart from their close relatives, the Adélies. The gentoo penguin also has a white "cap" extending from eye to eye on the top of its head. Gentoo penguins live on islands in the Southern Ocean.

- Macaroni penguins have long, golden head feathers. Early explorers of Southern Ocean islands who discovered these lively birds thought the head feathers resembled a fashionable hairstyle worn by "Macaroni Club" members in London. That's how the macaroni penguin got its name.

## It's a Baby Boom:

- At SeaWorld we install the penguin rookery or nesting area when the penguins are ready to breed. The birds immediately start building nests with the smooth river rocks that we provide the smaller species.

- Within two weeks, the first eggs are laid, as pairs often return to the same mates and nest sites annually.

- The Aviculture department prefer to leave the eggs and chicks with the parents, however, they will artificially incubate and hand rear a chick, if necessary.

- If a pair has a history of poor parenting or improper incubation, Aviculture might foster their egg to another pair who may have had an infertile egg, or place the egg in the incubator if suitable foster parents are not available.

- The king and emperor penguins do not build a nest like the smaller species do—they incubate their single egg on top of their feet.

- SeaWorld was the first place to recreate the Antarctic environment and the first place to breed emperor penguins outside of Antarctica.

# Other Birds

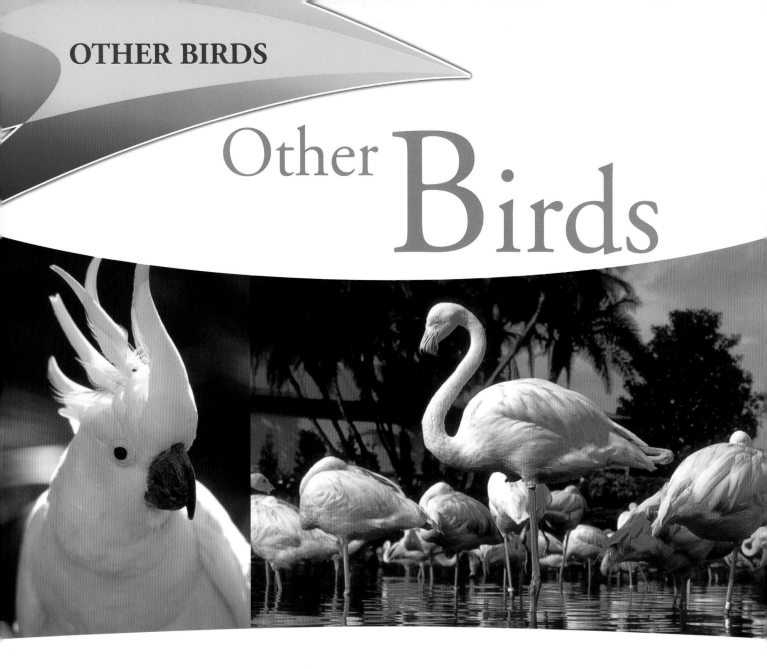

Birds of a feather flock together, and hundreds of bird species can be seen at SeaWorld. Here are some examples of the fascinating feathered friends that can be found throughout the parks:

**Macaws** are a large group of birds in the Psittacidae, or parrot, family. They range in size from the 30 cm (12 in.) Hahn's macaw (*Ara nobilis nobilis*) to the largest of all parrots, the hyacinth macaw (*Anodorhynchus hyacinthinus*) which can reach a size of around 102 cm (40 in.). The main natural enemy of macaws is the harpy eagle, but recently humans have devastated most macaw populations. In addition to damage done by rain forest habitat destruction, macaws are also hunted by humans for their plumage, meat, and for the exotic pet trade industry.

**Puffins** nest along the coastlines of Russia, Norway, Iceland, the British Isles, Western France, and Maine east to Greenland. Puffins can also be viewed by visiting SeaWorld Orlando,

SeaWorld San Diego, and SeaWorld San Antonio. During the breeding season their bills become vivid. Both parents incubate the egg and feed the chick. Puffins may dive deeper than 24 m (80 ft.) to catch fish. Their specialized bills are laced with sharp hooks that help hold fish. One puffin was seen with more than 60 fish in its bill at one time. In the air, puffins are powerful flyers, beating their wings 300 to 400 times a minute to achieve speeds up to 64 kph (40 mph).

A **flamingo's** pink or reddish feather, leg, and facial coloration come from a diet high in alpha and beta carotenoid pigments. The richest sources of carotenoids are found in algae and various insects that make up the staple of a flamingo's diet. Caribbean flamingos require about 270 g (9.5 oz.) of food per day. To feed, a flamingo stands in shallow water, hanging its head upside-down. The flamingo sweeps its head from side to side to filter the water or mud and collect its food.

**Pelicans** are easily recognized by their large bills which can hold more than 1.9 liters (2 gallons) of water. Two species of pelicans can be found in the United States—white pelicans (*Pelecanus erythrorhynchos*) and brown pelicans (*Pelecanus occidentalis*). White pelicans range in size from 140 to 179 cm (55–70 in.), have a wingspan up to 2.8 m (96 in.), and may weigh up to 13.6 kg (30 lb.). Pelicans are strong flyers, with some being able to travel up to 42 kph (26 mph).

The **Hawaiian nene goose** (*Branta sandvicensis*) is the official state bird of Hawaii. By 1951, the total wild population was estimated to be no more than 30 birds. Nenes were hunted for food and the introduction of non-native feral dogs and cats also contributed to their decline. Mongooses, introduced in 1883 to control non-native rats that plagued farmers, neither solved the rat problem nor remained in the sugarcane fields for long. Mongooses are a natural predator of ground nesting birds, and this soon included nene geese. SeaWorld is helping this endangered species through breeding programs and to date more than 80 nene geese have been hatched throughout the SeaWorld Adventure Parks.

The colorful **roseate spoonbill** (*Ajaia ajaja*) inhabits the southern United States to Argentina as well as the West Indies. Unlike the other spoonbills which are mostly white in color, roseate adults have pink plumage that deepens to red on the shoulders. Other spoonbills can be found in Europe, Asia, Africa, and Australia. Spoonbills prefer shallow fresh water areas and marshes.

**Bald eagles** (*Haliaeetus leucocephalus*) are a type of "fish" eagle but their diet also consists of birds and small mammals. In addition, bald eagles are scavengers that harass and steal fish from other birds. Because of its scavenging nature, Benjamin Franklin opposed the bald eagle as the national bird of the United States and proposed the wild turkey instead. Despite his argument that the wild turkey was more important to American settlers, the bald eagle was declared the national bird of the United States in 1782. Although protected by several laws, the bald eagle faced extinction from many human activities such as pesticide contamination and hunting for its feathers.

# Sea Turtles

Most scientists recognize eight species of these marine reptiles. Experts can identify each by the number and pattern of scutes (horny plates) on the carapace (top shell). Sea turtle species range in length from about 53 cm (21 in.) up to 1.9 m (6 ft.). Males and females are about the same size. Sea turtles share characteristics with other reptiles: they are ectothermic ("cold-blooded"), they breathe air, and have scaly skin. Sea turtles cannot retract their limbs or head into their shells as land turtles can.

Diets vary greatly among sea turtle species. Green (*Chelonia mydas*) and black sea turtles (*Chelonia agassizi*) feed on seagrasses and algae. Loggerheads' (*Caretta caretta*) and olive ridleys' (*Lepidochelys olivacea*) strong jaws can crush crabs, shrimps, and molluscs. Leatherbacks (*Dermochelys coriacea*) prey only on jellyfish and other soft-bodied animals.

In general, sea turtles do not come out onto land, except females when they nest. Most nest during the warmest months, returning to the same beaches year after year. A female sea turtle digs a pit in the sand using her hind flippers and deposits 50 to 200 eggs, each the size of a ping pong ball. The incubation period for most species is 45 to 70 days.

All eight sea turtle species are listed as either endangered or threatened. Despite several management measures to preserve sea turtles, their future is still in question, due to a number of natural and human-related factors such as hunting and pollution.

## Fast Facts:

* Sea turtles can stay under water as long as five hours. To conserve oxygen, their hearts can slow to one beat every nine minutes.

* Sea turtles are found in tropical and temperate seas throughout the world. Adults of most species inhabit shallow coastal waters. Some species migrate great distances from winter feeding grounds to summer nesting areas.

* Sea turtles' long, paddlelike flippers are adapted to locomotion in the water.

* One of SeaWorld's largest and most dramatic rescues was of 95 hypothermic green sea turtles from Florida's Indian River Lagoon. After about 10 weeks of rehabilitation, the turtles were released back in the same area that they were rescued.

# Clydesdales

There are at least 111 recognized breeds of domesticated horses, including Suffolks, thoroughbreds, quarterhorses, and Arabians. Of these, the Clydesdale is one of the largest and most well known.

The Clydesdale breed originated in the mid-1700s in Scotland, in the Clydesdale region of Lanarkshire. This region, along the banks of the River Clyde, contained rich farmland. According to legend, one of the dukes of Hamilton imported six black Flemish coach stallions from Flanders and made them available for breeding. Many of the horses sired from these stallions were progenitors of the Clydesdale breed today. Following contributions from Flemish and Frisian stallions, the definitive characteristics of the breed were fixed at the beginning of the eighteenth century. The Clydesdale breed was officially recognized in 1878.

## Fast Facts:

- At the SeaWorld and Busch Gardens Adventure Parks, Clydesdales are fed hay and feed. The feed is a mixture of beet pulp, oats, bran, minerals, salt, molasses and water. Each Clydesdale consumes approximately 19 liters (20 quarts) of feed, 18 to 23 kg (40–50 lb.) of hay, and 114 liters (30 gallons) of water every day.

- A male's average weight is 771 to 998 kg (1,700–2,200 lb.) while a female averages 680 to 771 kg (1,500–2,000 lb.).

# Rescue & Rehabilitation

Through the SeaWorld/Busch Gardens Animal Rescue and Rehabilitation Program our parks have rescued, treated, sheltered and released more than 100 species of stranded, sick and injured animals all around the world. It's one of the largest rescue programs of its kind anywhere in the world.

## Fast Facts:

* Since 1970, the parks have rescued more than 13,000 animals.

* The main objective of the Animal Rescue and Rehabilitation Program is to return rescued animals to the wild.

* The financial commitment to the Animal Rescue and Rehabilitation Program is estimated at more than one million dollars per year.

* Animals that have survived their illness or injury, but are determined non-releasable, have been adopted and given permanent homes by SeaWorld and Busch Gardens.

* Many of the animals that can be seen at SeaWorld, ranging from brown pelicans to endangered manatees and sea turtles, are examples of rescued animals that are given homes at SeaWorld parks.

* SeaWorld Orlando has released more than 500 endangered or threatened sea turtles and more than 140 endangered manatees through this program.

# CONSERVATION FUND

## Our roots...

The Anheuser-Busch Adventure Parks are world-renowned for providing up-close animal encounters and unparalleled entertainment experiences for more than 20 million guests each year. Perhaps less known is the parks' 50-year commitment to wildlife conservation, animal care, research and education.

Since the first park opened in 1958, Busch Gardens, SeaWorld and Discovery Cove have shared a common passion – animals. This passion is reflected throughout the parks' award-winning zoological habitats, innovative veterinary care, animal rescue and rehabilitation efforts, education programs and critical conservation initiatives worldwide.

This passion is shared not only by park staff but by millions of guests each year. Upon visiting an Anheuser-Busch Adventure Park, many guests are inspired to help protect the animals they encounter and get involved with wildlife conservation. The SeaWorld & Busch Gardens Conservation Fund was, in part, created to fulfill that desire.

## Habitat Protection

To save a species ultimately means saving its home – the place in which it seeks shelter, forages, breeds and raises young. For some animals, a habitat might be a one-acre tract while for others a massive, multinational expanse. Protecting and preserving these special places is a difficult yet critical conservation challenge and a key focus for the Fund.

## Conservation Education

Perhaps the most enduring and effective conservation investment is education. With the power to transform information into insight and awareness into action, conservation education is a cornerstone of the Fund. People of all ages, backgrounds and resources, once engaged, can overcome tremendous odds, reverse trends and help secure a sustainable future for wildlife.

In its first two years of operation, the SeaWorld & Busch Gardens Conservation Fund has granted $2 million to more than 100 projects around the world, from saving sea turtles in Costa Rica

# Who we are today...

Launched in 2003, the SeaWorld & Busch Gardens Conservation Fund was created with a dual-purpose:
1) provide guests with an easy, direct way to get involved and make a difference for wildlife and
2) strengthen and expand the parks' existing conservation efforts. A 501(c)(3) non-profit organization, the SeaWorld & Busch Gardens Conservation Fund invests its resources in four strategic areas: Habitat Protection, Conservation Education, Animal Rescue and Rehabilitation and Species Research.

# Get Involved!

The SeaWorld & Busch Gardens Conservation Fund accepts grant applications year-round. The Fund's Board of Directors convenes once a year to review and award grants. The deadline for submitting grant applications is December 1. Grant applications are available for download at *SWBG-ConservationFund.org*.

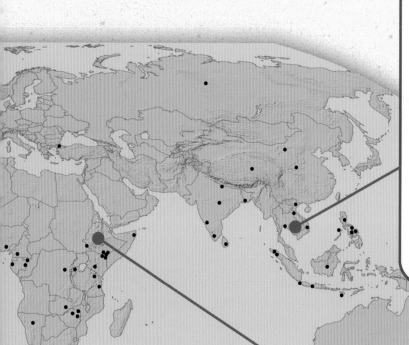

## Animal Rescue & Rehabilitation

In addition to natural events and catastrophes, everyday human activity can pose serious threats to wildlife. From oil spills and boat strikes to habitat loss and entanglement with potentially fatal debris, animals in crisis are sadly common worldwide. The Fund helps respond to such crisis situations.

## Species Research

Ranging from population surveys of endangered whales to behavioral studies of wild zebras, science-based species research equips wildlife conservationists, citizens, policy-makers and other stakeholders with an expanded knowledge of animals and their environment. Research findings can be applied to help resolve human-animal conflict and lead to sustainable conservation solutions – a critical goal of the Fund.

to protecting rhinos in Kenya to rescuing seabirds along the U. S. coast. Above is a map highlighting a few of these projects and the significant conservation benefits they are delivering.

# Up-Close Animal Encounters

Ever wanted to swim with a dolphin or dine next to dozens of sharks? The SeaWorld Adventure Parks and Discovery Cove offer awesome animal interactions that allows guests to get up close and personal with a variety of animals. SeaWorld also educates thousands of students and guests every year through school programs, guided tours and amazing Adventure Camps. Check out *SeaWorld.com*, *SeaWorld.org* and *DiscoveryCove.com* to learn more about these once-in-a-lifetime opportunities.